On Nana's Knees

Guiding Little Hearts Through God's Commandments

Shelda Mae

Illustrated By
Trevion Garland

TEACH Services, Inc.
P U B L I S H I N G
www.TEACHServices.com • (800) 367-1844

World rights reserved. This book or any portion thereof may not be copied or reproduced in any form or manner whatever, except as provided by law, without the written permission of the publisher, except by a reviewer who may quote brief passages in a review.

The author assumes full responsibility for the accuracy of all facts, cited quotations, and interpretations in this book and for use of illustrations and cited materials. The opinions expressed in this book are the author's personal views and interpretations, and do not necessarily reflect those of the publisher.

This book is provided with the understanding that the publisher is not engaged in giving spiritual, legal, medical, or other professional advice. If authoritative advice is needed, the reader should seek the counsel of a competent professional.

Copyright © 2025 Shelda Mae

Copyright © 2025 TEACH Services, Inc.

Published in Calhoun, Georgia, USA

ISBN-13: 978-1-4796-1907-8 (Paperback)

ISBN-13: 978-1-4796-1908-5 (ePub)

Library of Congress Control Number: 2025917417

All scripture quotations are taken from the King James Version.

This book is dedicated to my grandsons, Kamir and Zayden, and my children, MJ, Trey, Nyah, Chris, Ruth, and Malachi.

To my remarkable mother and greatest inspiration, thank you for showing me what it means to be a truly wonderful Nana.

Thou shalt have no other gods before me

Thou shalt not make unto thee any graven image

Thou shalt not take the name of the Lord thy God in vain

Remember the sabbath day, to keep it holy

Honor thy father and thy mother

Thou shalt not kill

Thou shalt not commit adultery

Thou shalt not steal

Thou shalt not bear false witness against thy neighbor

Thou shalt not covet

It's never too soon to teach a child God's rules to keep them safe, healthy, and happy.

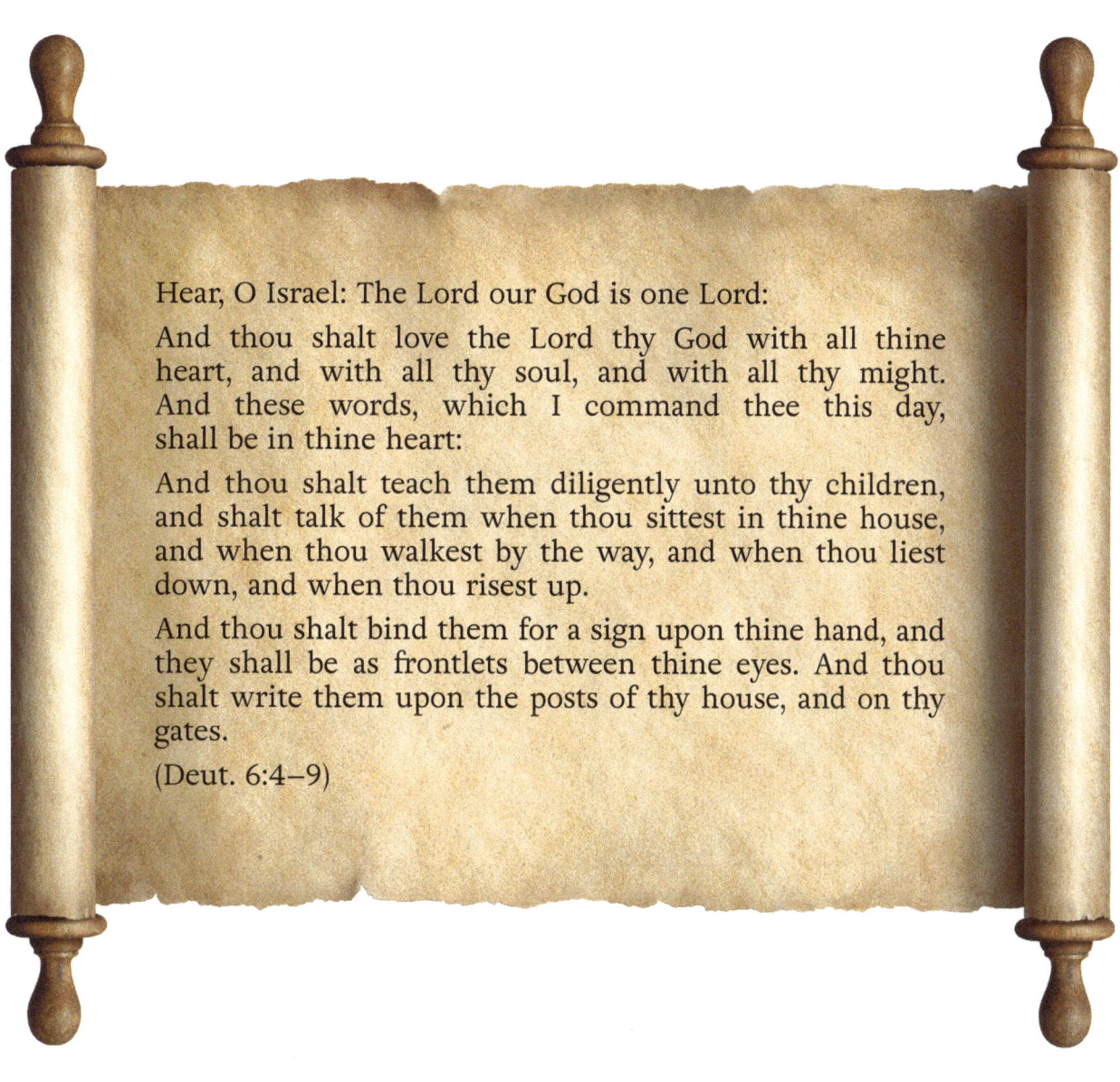

NANA

In North America ...

God's Rule #1

When Nana noticed I woke every morning first wanting my favorite art tool, she sat me on her knees and taught me God's first rule.

Nana said, "God is the only God, and you should love Him more than you love anything else, always putting Him first."

Now when I wake up, I say my prayers because I remember the first commandment's verse.

On Nana's knees,
I learn rules
like these:

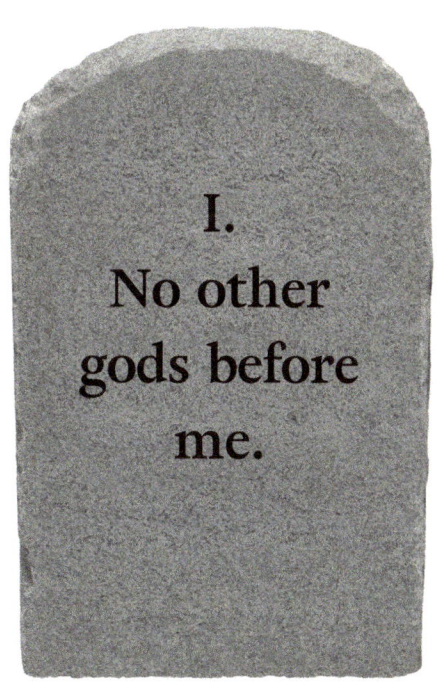

NANI

In India ...

God's Rule #2

Nani knows I love my teddy very much because I take him everywhere I go.

I've had him since I was a baby and will keep him as I grow.

When I keep being late for our family Bible study because I can't find my teddy's other shoe, Nani puts me on her knees and teaches me about God's rule number two.

Nani says I shouldn't allow anything to be more important than God and to worship Him only. When I showed Nani that I knew God's rule number two, she gave me some oatmeal and extra honey.

On Nana's knees,
I learn rules
like these:

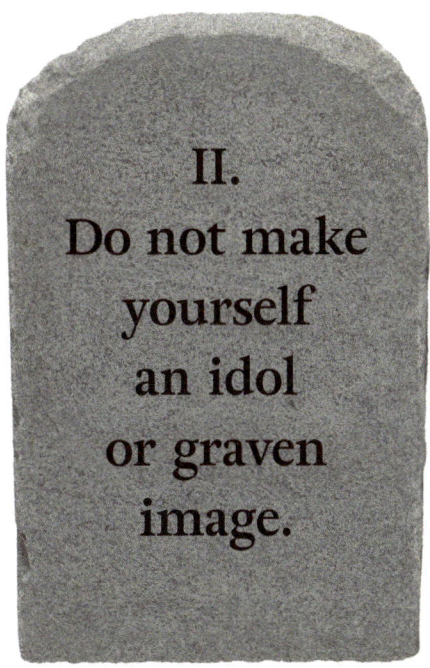

II. Do not make yourself an idol or graven image.

YAYA

In Spain ...

God's Rule #3

One day, Josiah keeps asking Jessie to read him his favorite book, but she is too busy.

When Josiah does not give up, Jessie becomes angry and yells, "Jesus! Leave me alone! I'm talking to my friend, Lizzy!"

Yaya heard Jessie and told her to come sit on her knee, so she can teach her about God's rule number three.

"Jessie, did you know that your name is very special," Yaya asks. "It means God has been gracious."

Yaya then asked Jessie, "Would it be nice if I yelled your name on a regular basis?"

"No Yaya, that would be mean and lame."

"That's right, and it's not nice to misuse Jesus' name—

We should keep God's name holy, by our words and actions, to show Him the respect He deserves."

Yaya smiled and said, "Always let what you do and how you speak honor our heavenly Father and keep calm Yaya's nerves."

On Nana's knees,

I learn rules

like these:

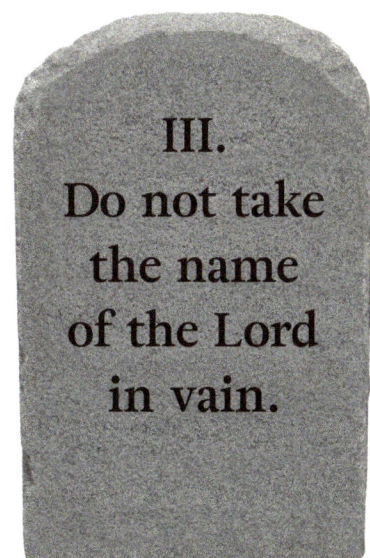

III. Do not take the name of the Lord in vain.

BIBI

In Africa ...

God's Rule #4

Zayden asks his Bibi, "Why do you go to church on Saturday with your church family?"

Bibi is happy to explain and graciously smiles at Zayden as she places him on her knee.

"Just like God worked hard for six days, and then He rested on day seven, we should also take a break from our work and play and give our hearts to God in heaven.

So let us keep rule number four, remember the Sabbath day, on day seven, and follow the example of our Father in heaven.

For obedience brings God's blessings near, as we embrace His love with hearts full of cheer."

"Thank you," Zayden said, "I will remember rule number four, the Sabbath day, a special day set apart, to rest and worship, come what may, and honor God's holy heart."

On Nana's knees, I learn rules like these:

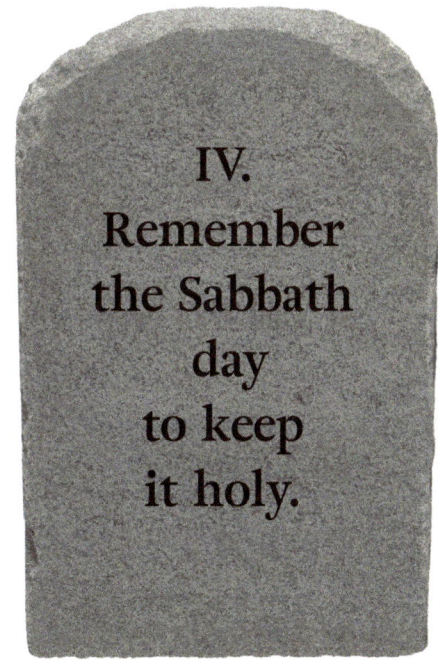

NONNA

In Italy ...

God's Rule #5

When Nonna heard me being disrespectful, she gently grabbed me and put me on her knee to teach me about rule number five and the importance of honoring my mommy and daddy.

"Listen well, my dear one, to the words I have to say, about the importance of honoring your mother and father every day.

Show them kindness and respect in everything you do, for they do their best to give you what you need and try to always be there for you.

Remember, honor is a gift, that we give to those we love, and when we honor our parents, God smiles on us from above."

I hugged my mom and dad, and told them I was sorry, and I want to obey, for they are special and dear to me, and to love and respect them always is the right way.

On Nana's knees,
I learn rules
like these:

OMA

In Germany ...

God's Rule #6

When Oma saw me get angry and kick my friend, Felix,
She put me on her knee to teach me about God's rule number six.
Oma said that God loves all His children, and in His eyes, we are all the same.
He created us to live and love, not to hurt or cause pain.
God says, "Thou shalt not kill," because He values every life of every kind.
To take someone's life is wrong, and those that do, in them His love He cannot find.
So, let's cherish and respect all lives and never harm or hurt anyone purposely.
For God's love is with us always, and He wants us to live in peace and harmony.

*On Nana's knees,
I learn rules
like these:*

BA

In Vietnam ...

God's Rule #7

Ba heard me crying in my room because my mom and dad got a divorce, and I just could not understand why my mom no longer loved my dad, Kevin. Ba told me to sit on her knee, so she could teach me all about God's rule number seven.

When two people find love, they may decide to get married one day. God said, "Thou shalt not commit adultery" to be married the right way. When you get married to that person, husband or wife, except for God, he or she becomes the most important person in your life.

This means we can't have any other boyfriends or girlfriends to love the way we do our spouse.

If we do, we hurt their feelings, and bring strife into the marriage and the house.

Marriage is a promise to cherish and love your husband or wife, come what may.

Even when troubles of all kinds may arise one day.

A husband and wife should always pray together and do right by one another, too.

They should also remember God's rule they committed to when they said, "I do."

On Nana's knees,
I learn rules
like these:

MAMIE

In France...

God's Rule #8

I told my Mamie that I like it when my little cousin comes to visit me, but I don't like it when he takes my toys… It makes me not feel so great.

Mamie put both my little cousin and me on her knees so she could talk to us about God's rule number eight.

When you play with others, always ask with a smile, if you can borrow their toys for a little while.

Return them when you're done and do so with care. This shows respect and is always fair.

Remember, stealing is never okay. It hurts others and leads us astray. Instead, we should practice honesty every day, and build a world for trust to stay.

On Nana's knees,
I learn rules
like these:

SOBO

In Japan...

God's Rule #9

I went to my Sobo to tell her Jack is a thief because he stole my money. Sobo asked me if I saw him take it, and I said, "No." Sobo then said, "I have a story to tell you, honey. It's about a very important rule you need to follow.

When I was little like you, I let my friend borrow my favorite toy. When it came up missing, I blamed her." My Sobo put me on her knees and taught me God's rule number nine: You shall not bear false witness against your neighbor.

I accused my friend of doing something wrong, and like you, I didn't have any proof or evidence. My friend's feelings were hurt, and she also felt betrayed. Especially when I found my toy had been misplaced, it was then forgiveness my heart conveyed.

When we lie, spread false information or rumors about someone else, it can hurt their reputation and create misunderstandings. We should always be honest and fair in our dealings with others. This keeps our relationships filled with kindness and respect for our sisters and brothers.

On Nana's knees, I learn rules like these:

IX.
Do not
lie or bear
false witness.

NAN

In Britain...

God's Rule #10

One day Nan took my big sister and me to the store to buy us a treat.
She bought Karah a new Barbie, and she bought me a baby doll with a car seat.
I wasn't happy with my new doll, and I threw a fit because I wanted Karah's Barbie.
Nan sat on a bench outside the store and put me on her knee.

Kiah, it's time for you to learn all about God's rule number ten: You shall not covet. This means we should not want what belongs to others, and we should be happy with what we have, even if it is just a puppet.

When we see our siblings or friends with toys, games, or other treats, we should be happy for them and not fill our hearts with envy or sadness. Instead, we should be grateful for what we have and fill our hearts with lots of thanks and gladness. So little ones, remember this commandment well, to be content and grateful, as the Bible does tell. For when we cherish what we have each day, we'll find true happiness along life's way.

On Nana's knees,
I learn rules
like these:

LOVE GOD

(see also Deut. 5:7–15)

I.

Thou shalt have no other gods before me. (Exod. 20:3)

II.

Thou shalt not make unto thee any graven image, or any likeness of any thing that is in heaven above, or that is in the earth beneath, or that is in the water under the earth. Thou shalt not bow down thyself to them, nor serve them: for I the Lord thy God am a jealous God, visiting the iniquity of the fathers upon the children unto the third and fourth generation of them that hate me; And shewing mercy unto thousands of them that love me, and keep my commandments. (Exod. 20:4–6)

III.

Thou shalt not take the name of the Lord thy God in vain; for the Lord will not hold him guiltless that taketh his name in vain. (Exod. 20:7)

IV.

Remember the sabbath day, to keep it holy. Six days shalt thou labour, and do all thy work:

But the seventh day is the sabbath of the Lord thy God: in it thou shalt not do any work, thou, nor thy son, nor thy daughter, thy manservant, nor thy maidservant, nor thy cattle, nor thy stranger that is within thy gates: For in six days the Lord made heaven and earth, the sea, and all that in them is, and rested the seventh day: wherefore the Lord blessed the sabbath day, and hallowed it. (Exod. 20:8–11)

V.

Honour thy father and thy mother: that thy days may be long upon the land which the Lord thy God giveth thee. (Exod. 20:12)

VI.

Thou shalt not kill. (Exod. 20:13)

VII.

Thou shalt not commit adultery. (Exod. 20:14)

VIII.

Thou shalt not steal. (Exod. 20:15)

IX.

Thou shalt not bear false witness against thy neighbour. (Exod. 20:16)

X.

Thou shalt not covet thy neighbour's house, thou shalt not covet thy neighbour's wife, nor his manservant, nor his maidservant, nor his ox, nor his ass, nor any thing that is thy neighbour's. (Exod. 20:17)

"Nana" in Ten Different Languages

Name	Place
Nana	America
Nani	India
Yaya	Spain
Bibi	Africa
Nonna	Italy
Oma	Germany
Bà	Vietnam
Mamie	France
Sobo	Japan
Nan	Britain

Vocabulary Chart

Word(s)	Rule #	Meaning
Idol	2	a statue or other object people worship like a god
Graven	2	carved or sculpted
Vain	3	false or worthless
Honor	5	respect and obey
Adultery	7	breaking wedding vows
False Witness	9	words that are not true
Covet	10	selfishly want what belongs to others

TEACH Services, Inc.
P U B L I S H I N G

We invite you to view the complete
selection of titles we publish at:
www.TEACHServices.com

We encourage you to write us
with your thoughts about this,
or any other book we publish at:
info@TEACHServices.com

TEACH Services' titles may be purchased in
bulk quantities for educational, fund-raising,
business, or promotional use.
bulksales@TEACHServices.com

Finally, if you are interested in seeing
your own book in print, please contact us at:
publishing@TEACHServices.com

We are happy to review your manuscript at no charge.

www.ingramcontent.com/pod-product-compliance
Lightning Source LLC
Chambersburg PA
CBHW061119170426
43200CB00023B/2999